IRAN
IRGC'S RISING DRONE THREAT

A DESPERATE REGIME'S PLOY
TO PROJECT POWER, INCITE WAR

IRAN: IRGC's Rising Drone Threat
A Desperate Regime's Ploy to Project Power, Incite War

First published in 2021 by
National Council of Resistance of Iran - U.S. Representative Office (NCRI-US),
1747 Pennsylvania Ave., NW, Suite 1125, Washington, DC 20006

ISBN-10 (paperback): 1-944942-46-7
ISBN-13 (paperback): 978-1-944942-46-5

ISBN-10 (e-book): 1-944942-47-5
ISBN-13 (e-book): 978-1-944942-47-2

ISBN-10 (audiobook): 1-944942-48-3
ISBN-13 (audiobook): 978-1-944942-48-9

Library of Congress Control Number: 2021951807

Library of Congress Cataloging-in-Publication Data

National Council of Resistance of Iran - U.S. Representative Office.

IRAN: IRGC's Rising Drone Threat
1. Iran. 2. Drones. 3. UAV. 4. Terrorism. 5. Middle East.

First Edition: December 2021
Printed in the United States of America

TABLE OF CONTENTS

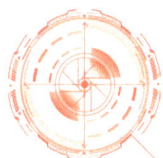

FOREWORD
by General James T. Conway

The Iranian development of a full-scale UAV and armed drone program represents an increased danger to U.S. troops in the Middle East — and takes the conflict(s) there to the next level of sophistication. For the past few decades, the Iranian Air Force has become sorely outdated — based on sanctions and the resulting inability to upgrade to a coherent capability. The Iranian counter has been to reverse-engineer, buy, or steal drone technology that gives them power projection beyond their borders — at fractional cost in terms of logistics and support requirements. The following pages describe in detail the massive investment that has gone into the Iranian drone effort. The civilized world, once again, is indebted to the MEK movement for "raising the curtain" on projects within Iran that are fully intended to raise havoc in the region.

The regime has learned much over the past 20 years observing the value and effectiveness of the U.S. UAV fleet — to include the targeted death of Qassem Soleimani. Armed drones can be used to attack military installations, attack critical infrastructure nodes, and attempt to assassinate high level political figures. Iran — or its proxies — have done all these things within the past six months! Intelligence agencies, the world over, would do well to use the information contained in this document to cross-reference what they think they already know about this growing challenge.

Can the threat be reduced or eliminated? Are there more effective counter-measures that can be employed to address this new and deadly capability?   Must we always surrender the initiative to the Iranians as to when and where? These and other questions need to be answered — sooner rather than later — by the U.S. and partner nations. In the meantime, what should scare us all, is the possession of these sophisticated weapons in the hands of a regime that considers "terrorism" an element of its national power.

— Gen. James T. Conway,
USMC (Ret) was the 34th Commandant of the U.S. Marine Corps

PREFACE
by Ambassador
Robert G. Joseph

This report provides a wealth of information on Iran's drone program, highlighting the use of unmanned aerial vehicles (UAVs) by the IRGC Quds force to conduct regional aggression and export terrorism. Published by the National Council of Resistance of Iran (NCRI), the report is informed by numerous sources inside Iran, primarily members of the People's Mujahedeen of Iran (MEK) who, at risk of their own lives, have worked to expose from within the true nature of the religious dictatorship that seeks to destabilize the region through force while brutally repressing its own people, the first and foremost victims of the regime.

For over twenty years, the NCRI has been an invaluable source of information and insightful analysis on the intentions, capabilities, and actions of the Iranian regime. Through its reports, briefings, and public presentations, the NCRI has provided a unique and proven perspective on a broad range of the regime's illicit programs and malign activities inside and outside of Iran. In 2002, the NCRI presented the first comprehensive view of Iran's nuclear weapons program, identifying the key facilities of that program. Since then, the NCRI has made public the main pillars underpinning the regime. These include the expansive presence and central role of the IRGC in foreign aggression and internal repression; the pervasive corruption of the mullahs who have stolen the wealth of the nation and who rule through torture and murder; and the regime's conduct and sponsorship of terrorism, both through direct actions and proxies. Additional NCRI publications have focused on advanced military capabilities, including the scale and scope of Iran's ballistic missile force and, with this publication, the regime's investment in the drone program which provides one of the primary weapons for use against its neighbors and in terrorist operations.

The high value placed on drones by the regime is reflected in the amount of resources it has committed to acquiring a large and sophisticated UAV arsenal, both through domestic production and through the illicit procurement of advanced components abroad. It is also reflected in the increased employment of drones to advance its goals through armed attacks against its neighbors and domestic opponents. These attacks have been conducted both directly, by the Quds Force, and through the provision of drones to proxy groups and terrorist organizations. They have involved numerous operations in Syria to assist the Assad regime in its war against its own people, as well as in Iraq, Lebanon, Yemen, and in the Kurdish regions of Iran. The toll of civilian deaths from these attacks has not been calculated.

Drones have substantial tactical value for the regime, providing affordable operational flexibility in the absence of a competent and effective air force. But the principal strategic value of UAVs to the regime is best understood in the broader geostrategic context. Having lost all legitimacy at home, the regime sees its very survival as a function of its ability to export its influence and ideology outside of Iran. Drones, like ballistic missiles, serve this purpose by providing a means of intimidation and attack. For this reason, the regime will never give up this capability. Instead, it will continue to expand its drone capabilities and will increase the frequency of their use. This must be a factor in the design of policies and capabilities intended to counter Iran's aggression.

As the Biden administration resumed talks in Vienna in its quixotic attempt to restore the 2015 nuclear accord, the Joint Comprehensive Plan of Action (JCPOA), it should keep in mind the lessons and unintended consequences of that agreement, especially the lifting of sanctions and providing the regime with billions of dollars to devote to weapon systems such as drones. The expectations of the Obama-Biden administration have been proven to be both false and dangerous.

The JCPOA was portrayed as a means to engineer positive change inside Iran by strengthening the so-called moderate faction, supposedly headed by then President Rouhani, against the hardliners. The thought was that the hundreds of billions of dollars Iran would receive from sanctions relief would be used to improve its economy, which in turn would lead to political moderation and Iran serving as a stabilizing force in the region. Even putting aside the false premise that such a division exists in a governing elite selected under the rules of the religious dictatorship, we now know what actually happened to the windfall of cash delivered to the regime. The money that was not siphoned off through corruption was used to inflame Sunni–Shiite divisions and provoke instability throughout the region. The IRGC and the military acquired even more deadly arsenals of missiles, drones and other weapons used to support the murderous Assad regime, the Houthis, and others, including Iran's terrorist proxies.

In an effort to justify the decision to rejoin the JCPOA, the Biden administration has disparaged as a failure the maximum-pressure policy of its predecessor. Yet the policy was having exactly the intended effect. The imposition of broad sanctions on Iran, including restrictions on its ability to use the global banking system, was having a devastating impact on the economy. Strikes in key sectors broke out, along with large-scale demonstrations that threatened the very foundation of the regime. This movement for change was met with barbarity. In late 2019 alone, over 1,500 demonstrators were murdered in the streets.

The administration's myopic focus on rejoining the JCPOA also ignores the fundamental changes in the security environment of the Gulf region since 2015. American allies from Jerusalem to Riyadh understand the nature of the Tehran regime and are working together to confront the threat. The concessions that the Biden administration is reportedly willing to make to return to the nuclear agreement will directly undercut the position of our allies, to the long-term strategic detriment of our national interests.

The Biden administration, in rejecting the above concerns, has stated that rejoining the JCPOA is only the first step; a step that will be followed by negotiations to address the agreement's flaws, such as its failure to limit ballistic missiles, and curb Iran's malign behavior in the region. These are the same objectives that were sought in the original negotiations but abandoned when the Supreme Leader ruled them out. That position has not changed, and there is no indication that it will. When the U.S. lifts sanctions as a condition of rejoining the agreement, it will be the last step, not the first step. Iran will have again achieved its objectives. And the U.S. will have again paid a high price for a bad deal — a price that includes more missiles, more drones, and more aggression.

The illusion that Iran can serve as a stabilizing force in the region can only be explained as the triumph of hope over experience. But perhaps the greatest fallacy of the Biden approach is the belief that it can negotiate in good faith with the regime and that, if there is an agreement, Iran will live up to its commitments. On this score, people matter as much, if not more, than stated policy. And the new team, installed by the Supreme Leader after fraudulent elections in June, makes evident that the underlying assumptions of the Biden strategy will only produce further failure and further loss to vital U.S. interests.

Perhaps for this reason, relatively little official attention has been devoted to the rogue's gallery that constitutes the new Iranian leadership, at least ten of whom are today sanctioned by the US., Europe and the UN. First and foremost, the list includes Ebrahim Raisi, the new president, who served as a member of the Tehran death committee in the murder of thousands of political prisoners in 1988. These political executions, aimed primarily at the MEK, were widely condemned, and for decades, human rights groups have called for an investigation into Raisi's part in the killings. In 2019, the U.S. condemned Raisi's appointment as the head of Iran's judiciary and sanctioned him, citing his role in the mass executions and his participation in the brutal repression of protesters following the 2009 sham election. The Iranian regime continues to this day to conceal its crimes against humanity. Raisi speaks only of his pride in having served his Supreme Leader.

The selection of Raisi as president reflects the moral bankruptcy of the mullahs and the weakness of the regime's leaders, and most of all their fear of the peoples' calls for justice. Today, the mullahs' desperation is palpable — we can see it in the calls across Iran for an end to the intolerant and corrupt regime. The people have seen their beloved country become a prison to those inside and a pariah to those on the outside. And the regime's response — not reform but more repression — will accelerate the certainty of its destruction. Policies of appeasement must be rejected as they will only serve to prolong the life of the regime, its external aggression and its domestic brutality.

— Ambassador Robert Joseph, Ph.D.,
is a former Under Secretary of State for Arms Control and
International Security and Special Envoy for Nonproliferation

SUMMARY

In that the clerical regime in Iran lacks the military capability to build advanced weaponry, it has resorted to the production of weapons and equipment that can be used for terrorist and war-mongering activities intended to advance its policy of creating crises and fueling terrorism. One such weapon, in the production and export of which the regime has invested heavily in recent years, is a variety of drones, or unmanned aerial vehicles (UAVs).

This manuscript offers a review of the most important organs of production, use and export of UAVs by the regime, and in particular the Islamic Revolutionary Guard Corps (IRGC).

In the first chapter, entitled "Production of UAVs," the history of the IRGC's production of the earliest types of UAVs during the Iran-Iraq War is reviewed, after which the Quds Air Industries, affiliated with the Air Industries Organization in the Ministry of Defense, and 7 other related bodies became involved in such production. Next, the ways in which equipment is smuggled from abroad and the production of various parts are explained. A variety of UAVs used by the IRGC to ignite war and terrorism are then introduced.

The second chapter, entitled "Utilization of UAVs," offers a brief overview of how the IRGC has used drones historically, and outlines the various organs that employ UAVs. Among them is the UAV Command under the IRGC Aerospace Force, which has various UAV centers across Iran. It is the most important entity for training and using UAVs. Other military and law enforcement agencies that utilize UAVs are also named in this chapter.

In the third chapter, entitled "Using UAVs to incite war and terrorism," the utilization of UAVs for the advancement of terrorist policies and regional meddling by the IRGC's Quds Force is discussed. The Quds Force Intelligence and Training directorates have dedicated certain sections to the production as well as training and export of UAVs to other countries in the region. The IRGC's drone command center was directly involved in the attack on the Saudi Aramco oil refinery. The IRGC also continues to export drones to Syria, Iraq, Lebanon and Yemen. UAV parts are flown to these countries in IRGC planes as well as shipped through land crossings, and are subsequently assembled in the host countries. Local mercenaries from these countries receive training at IRGC Aerospace Force locations in Iran.

The findings make clear that the reason for the IRGC's focus on the production and use of drones lies in the fundamental military weaknesses of the regime when it comes to modern warfare. On the other hand, the IRGC has used drones, much like its missile program, as an instrument to instigate conflict and terrorism in the region in order to keep the clerical dictatorship in power.

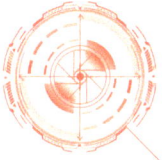

INTRODUCTION

The IRGC currently uses UAVs to create crisis and export terrorism on a wide scale in regional countries. It also relies on drones as propaganda tools to convey an undeserved impression of military prowess. This report, based on information obtained from the network inside Iran of the main Iranian opposition, the People's Mojahedin Organization of Iran (PMOI), also referred to as the Mujahedin-e Khalq (MEK), deals with the main entities involved in the production of UAVs, as well as the organs that use them.

The military apparatus of the clerical regime, especially the IRGC, lacks a reliable conventional air force. To compensate for this fundamental weakness, and in addition to its efforts to produce missiles, the regime has resorted to manufacturing drones and assembling an array of entities to use on the ground to shore up its policy of exporting terror and warmongering in the Middle East.

Tehran stepping up UAV production and utilization: The Iranian regime's Supreme Leader Ali Khamenei[1] and Foreign Minister Hossein Amir-Abdollahian have both said that they pursue their foreign policy objectives in the "theater," referring to regional meddling, including terrorist acts involving the firing of missiles and drones by Quds Force mercenaries.[2]

Brigadier General Amir Ali Hajizadeh, commander of the IRGC Aerospace Force, said in an interview on August 22, 2021 regarding Ali Khamenei's position on drones: "At some point, former Aerospace commanders

---

1   "Quds Force is the most important instrument for prevention of passive diplomacy in west of Asia," *International Quran News Agency,* May 2, 2021, https://iqna.ir/fa/news/3968811/

2   "Amir-Abdollahian: Ashura taught us that diplomacy and arena are two arms of realizing our national interests," *Fars News Agency,* August 22, 2021, https://www.farsnews.ir/news/14000531000677/

considered building aircraft, but [Khamenei] said, 'That is the Army's job. You should stick to building missiles and drones.'"[3]

The clerical regime has adopted this approach to carry out the maximum level of terrorism and destabilizing activities while paying the least political and military price. One example is the attack on the Aramco refinery in Saudi Arabia on September 14, 2019, using rockets and unmanned aerial vehicles (UAVs), for which the IRGC never accepted responsibility. This policy of plausible deniability is also evident in the use of UAVs by proxy forces affiliated with the IRGC, and underscores the political illegitimacy of these actions and the regime's political weakness in the international and regional arenas.

Drones require the least military expertise and funding compared to other weapons. Still, Tehran is unable to produce many of the parts key to UAV production and smuggles them in from abroad.

To obscure the weakness of its Air Force, the clerical regime ridiculously claims to be the fifth UAV power in the world. Brigadier General Afshin Khajehfard, head of the Ministry of Defense's Air Industries Organization, claimed on August 22, 2020, that "International organizations that assess the air combat capability have ranked Iran fifth in the field of UAVs or drones."[4]

Regional meddling and drone attacks have intensified during Raisi's presidency: Khamenei installed Ebrahim Raisi as the president of the regime after sham elections in order to close ranks and prevent more fissures within the ruling apparatus. The leaders of the proxy groups affiliated with the IRGC Quds Force, including Hezbollah in Lebanon, the Houthis in Yemen, Islamic Jihad and Hamas, and al-Najba in Iraq, congratulated the regime on the presidency of Raisi. He reciprocated by sending messages emphasizing the regime's support for all of them.

During the first three months of Raisi's tenure, the IRGC's Quds Force escalated its drone attacks. One example is the drone strike by Iraqi

---

3   "Sardar Hajizadeh: In drone, electronic warfare, and radar arenas, we are a world power," *Tasnim News Agency,* August 22, 2021, https://www.tasnimnews.com/fa/news/1400/05/31/2558566/

4   "Iran is fifth in the world in manufacturing UAVs," *Young Journalists Club,* August 22, 2021, https://www.yjc.news/fa/news/7466875/

militia affiliated with the IRGC's Quds Force on the Al-Tanf base in Syria on October 20, 2021. The *Washington Post* reported on October 24, 2021: "The latest example of how the drone battlefield is getting more even comes from a small U.S. outpost in the Syrian desert near the Iraqi border known as Tanf. The perpetrator was almost certainly one of the Iraqi Shiite militias that have targeted U.S. bases for years with mortar and rocket fire."[5]

Bloomberg wrote on October 21, 2021: "There are two reasons to suspect Iran's involvement. First, the proliferation of these crude, kamikaze drones is part of the Islamic Republic's regional strategy ... says David Schenker, a senior fellow at the Washington Institute for Near East Policy and a former assistant secretary of state for Near East Affairs."[6]

Condemnations of IRGC drone strikes by the international community: The regime's provocative terrorist acts accompanied by drone strikes or rocket attacks, have triggered international condemnation. For example, in June 2020, in a report to the Security Council on drone strikes on Saudi Arabia, UN Secretary General Antonio Guterres pointed to the Iranian regime: "The Secretariat assesses that the cruise missiles and/or parts thereof used in the four attacks are of Iranian origin," Guterres wrote.[7] Guterres also said that drones used in the May and September attacks were "of Iranian origin," adding that the United Nations had observed that some items in the two U.S. seizures "were identical or similar" to those found in the debris of the cruise missiles and the drones used in the 2019 attacks on Saudi Arabia.[8]

After the drone attack on the Mercer Street tanker, carried out by the IRGC in the Sea of Oman on July 29, 2021, Britain held the Iranian regime responsible for the attack. Barbara Woodward, Permanent Representative

---

5   Eli Lake, "How Iran is Leveling the Drone Battlefield," *The Washington Post*, October 24, 2021, https://www. washingtonpost.com/enterprise/vitality/how-iran-isleveling-the-drone-battlefield/2021/10/21/d179ba4a-32cb-11ec-8036-7db255bff176_story.html.

6   Eli Lake, "How Iran Is Leveling the Drone Battlefield," *Bloomberg*, October 21, 2021, https://www.bloomberg.com/opinion/articles/2021-10-21/attack-on-u-s-base-shows-how-iran-is-leveling-drone-battlefield.

7   "Weapons used against Saudi Arabia were 'of Iranian origin', UN says." *France 24*, June 13, 2020, https://www.france24.com/en/20200613-weapons-used-against-saudi-arabia-were-of-iranian-origin-un-says.

8   Michelle Nichols, "Arms Seized by U.S., missiles used to attack Saudi Arabia 'of Iranian origin': U.N." *Reuters*, June 11, 2020, https://www.reuters.com/article/us-iran-usa-un/arms-seized-by-u-s-missiles-used-to-attack-saudi-arabia-of-iranian-origin-u-n-idUSKBN23J08C.

of the United Kingdom to the United Nations told reporters on August, 6, 2021 that "the UK knows that Iran was responsible" for the attack against the MV Mercer Street vessel. Woodward said, "we know it was deliberate and targeted…the evidence, we are confident — based on our assessment of the debris that was recovered from the MV Mercer Street — that the system used in the attack was an Iranian Shahed-136 UAV, and these are manufactured only in Iran."[9]

In a press release on August 6, 2021, U.S. Central Command issued its findings on the investigation into the attack saying, "U.S. experts concluded based on the evidence that this UAV was produced in Iran."[10]

In addition, Radio Farda wrote on August 3, 2021: "NATO and the European Union also joined the United States and Britain in criticizing Iran for last week's drone strike on an oil tanker in the Sea of Oman, urging Iran to honor its international obligations."[11]

The North Atlantic Treaty Organization (NATO) condemned the attack and warned the regime to respect international law.[12] The European Union also condemned the attack as "unacceptable."[13] Two crew members, one British and one Romanian, were killed. Acting Deputy Spokesperson at NATO, Dylan White, said on behalf of the 30 member states of the organization, that NATO joined the US, British and Romanian governments in "strongly condemning the recent fatal attack on the MV Mercer Street off the coast of Oman, and express condolences to Romania and the United Kingdom."[14]

9   United Nations, "United Kingdom on Iran — Security Council Media Stakeout," YouTube, August 6, 2021, https://www. youtube.com/watch?v=wS6NcNZr29g.

10   "U.S. Central Command Statement on the Investigation into the Attack on the Motor Tanker Mercer Street," CENTCOM, August 6, 2021, https://www.centcom.mil/MEDIA/PRESS-RELEASES/Press-Release-View/Article/2722418/us-central-command-statement-on-the-investigation-into-the-attack-on-the-motor.

11   "NATO and EU condemn tanker attack; NATO warns Iran," Radio Farda, August 3, 2021, https://www.radiofarda.com/a/nato-warns-iran-on-mercer-street/31391873.html

12   "Statement by the Acting NATO Spokesperson on the Mercer Street vessel attack," North Atlantic Treaty Organization, August 3, 2021, https://www.nato.int/cps/en/natohq/news_186010.htm.

13   "Mercer Street Attack: Declaration by the High Representative on behalf of the European Union on the attack of 29 July on a merchant vessel off the coast of Oman." Council of the European Union, August 8, 2021, https://www.consilium.europa.eu/en/press/press-releases/2021/08/08/mercer-street-attack-declaration-by-the-high-representative-on-behalf-of-the-european-union-on-the-attack-of-29-july-on-a-merchant-vessel-off-the-coast-of-oman.

14   Dylan White (@dylanpwhite), Twitter, August 3, 2021, https://twitter.com/dylanpwhite/status/1422501665492570166.

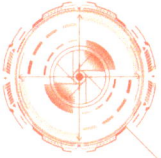

1. PRODUCTION OF UAVs

1.1. History of Iran regime's UAV production

To produce UAVs, the clerical regime smuggles some of the main parts, such as engines and electronic components, from foreign countries; other required components are produced in various industries within Iran.

According to our sources, 8 industries are responsible for manufacturing UAVs. Some operate under the Aviation Industries Organization of the Ministry of Defense, including Quds Air Industries, Iran Aircraft Manufacturing (HESA), Fajr Industries, and Basir Industries. Other sections of these complexes are affiliated with the IRGC Aerospace Force, the regime's various armed forces, or operate under the guise of private institutions.

The Quds Air Industries was established in 1985 as a unit in what was then the IRGC Ministry to produce the earliest and most basic types of UAVs. Since 1992, when the IRGC Ministry and the Ministry of Defense were merged, this body has been operating as a subset of the Defense Industries Organization. In 1998, Quds Air Industries was transferred from the Defense Industries Organization to the Aviation Industries Organization.

Hence, the primary entity currently involved in the manufacture of UAVs within the regime is the Quds Air Industries, which is a subset of the Aviation Industries Organization, itself operating under the umbrella of the Ministry of Defense. Quds Air Industries produces UAVs for the entire armed forces, especially for use by the UAV unit (group) in the IRGC Air Force. In addition, other regime organs have also been involved in the production of UAVs, typically using the factories under their control to do so. Some other organs have a complementary role in UAV production with Quds Air Industries, including the IRGC Aerospace Force, the IRGC Ground Forces, the Army's Air Force, and the Army's Ground Forces.

1.2. Aviation Industries Organization

The network for manufacturing UAVs and their related equipment and materials is organized under the auspices of the Aviation Industries Organization in the Ministry of Defense, and constitutes an important part of this industry. Out of the set of 7 organs that exist under the Aviation Industries Organization, the Quds Aviation Industries, Fajr Industries, and parts of the Basir, Aircraft Manufacturing Industries of Iran, and Aviation Industries of Iran are dedicated to the production of UAVs and related equipment.

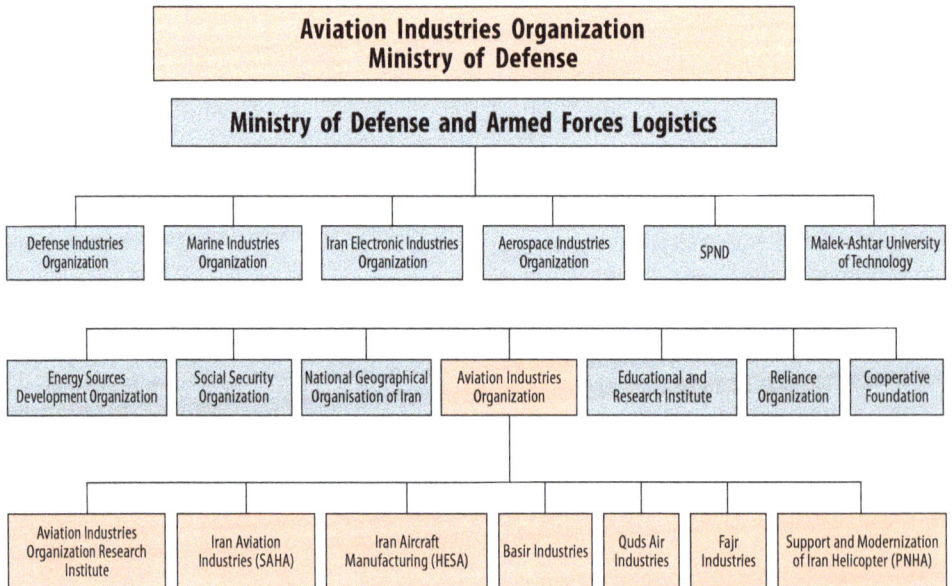

The organizational chart of the Aviation Industries Organization in the Ministry of Defense.

Other subdivisions of the Aviation Industries Organization that manufacture other products are Saha (Iranian Aviation Industry), HESA (Iran Aircraft Manufacturing) as well as Penha (Support and Renovation of Iranian Helicopters). They are involved in the repair and modernization of old military aircraft and helicopters left from the Shah's era, as well as the construction of some of the associated parts. Hence, the Ministry of Defense clearly does not currently have the capabilities to build aircraft or helicopters.

The headquarters of the Aviation Industries Organization is located at Qarani St., between Baradaran Shadab St. and Arak St. The current commander of this organization is (Amir) Afshin Khajehfard.

1.3. Quds Air Industries

Quds Air Industries operates under the Aviation Industries Organization of the Ministry of Defense. It changed its name to "Light Aircraft Design and Construction Industries" on December 13, 2019. The headquarters is located at km 4 of the Tehran-Karaj Expressway and is adjacent to the IRGC's Ghadr Airbase at Mehrabad Airport.

In addition to producing drones, Quds Air Industries designs and offers after-sales service for various types of drones and UAVs for reconnaissance, and kamikaze attacks as well as thermal drones; production and improvement of propellers, parachutes, and automatic and non-automatic landing parachutes; design and construction of ground control stations (GCS), electronic flight systems, aerial imaging, targeting, and optical tracking and ionization. Many of the staff at this organization are also employed in the Hemmat Missile Industries. The aircraft produced by this facility are sent to countries like Pakistan, Venezuela, some African nations, Hezbollah in Lebanon, the Houthis in Yemen, and to Syria and Iraq.

The current board of directors of this company is comprised of:

- Seyed Hojjatollah Qureishi (ID # 59298694141), the main member and chairman of the board

- Ghasem Damavandian (ID # 00529444492), permanent member and managing director
- Reza Khaki (ID # 1199127777), permanent member
- Hamid Reza Sharifi Tehrani (ID # 1285834070), permanent member
- Majid Reza Niazi Angili (ID # 0030171628), permanent member
- Vali Arlanizadeh (ID # 2802738003)

The departmental sections of the Quds Air Industry include:

- Executive Office
- Mechanical Department: Aircraft assembly unit (fuselage, engine, launcher)
- Electronics Department: Including administration, photography and cameras, navigation
- Finance Department: Budget division
- Administrative Department: Human resources
- Commercial Department: Aircraft sales

Other sections include the Design and Planning Department, Political Ideology, Information Protection, and Education Management (which reports to the Executive Office).

The aircraft manufactured in these industries are taken to two locations for final checks and test flights. One is located in the Semnan desert, and the other is located on the Old Qom-Tehran road (at 6 to 7 km mark from Qom to Tehran), where a sign for "Quds Air Industry" has been installed. Starting from this point and 20–25 km east is the area for test flights.

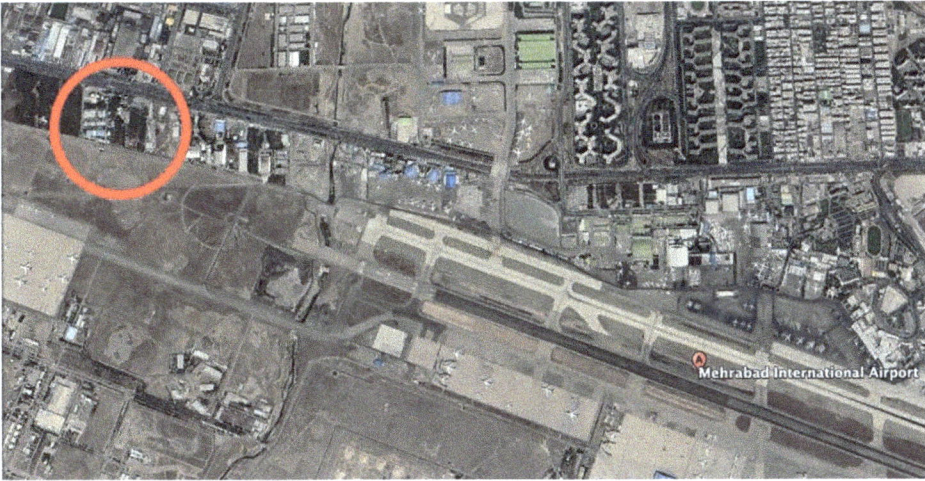

Quds Air Industries near Mehrabad Airport in Tehran

Quds Air Industries of the Defense Ministry

1- New administrative bldg.; 2- Design center; 3- Assembly units; 4- Computer department; 5- Final testing department

Quds Air Industries' main entrance

1.4. Fajr Aerospace and Composite Materials Industries

Fajr Aerospace and Composite Materials Industries is one of the factories controlled by the Aviation Industries Organization of the Ministry of Defense. It produces small single-engine aircraft, as well as some materials and parts related to UAVs. Fajr Industries is located next to Quds Air Industries on the Karaj Expressway.

Fajr Industries located next to Quds Air Industries

1.5. Iran Aircraft Manufacturing Company (HESA)

This company is one of the largest subsidiaries of the Aviation Industries Organization of the Ministry of Defense. It is located in Shahin Shahr, Isfahan. In addition to manufacturing aircraft parts, it is also involved in the construction of UAVs and their components. The so-called Ababil UAV, a smaller type of drone, was first built by this company. Its current head is Hamid Reza Nouri.

HESA in Shahin Shar, Isfahan

1.6. Basir Industries

Basir Industries is a subsidiary of the Aviation Industries Organization of the Ministry of Defense. It produces various parts and components for the aerospace and marine industries, including the production of small batteries for UAVs and diesel engines for IRGC speedboats. This company is located at km 1 of the Babol — Amol highway.

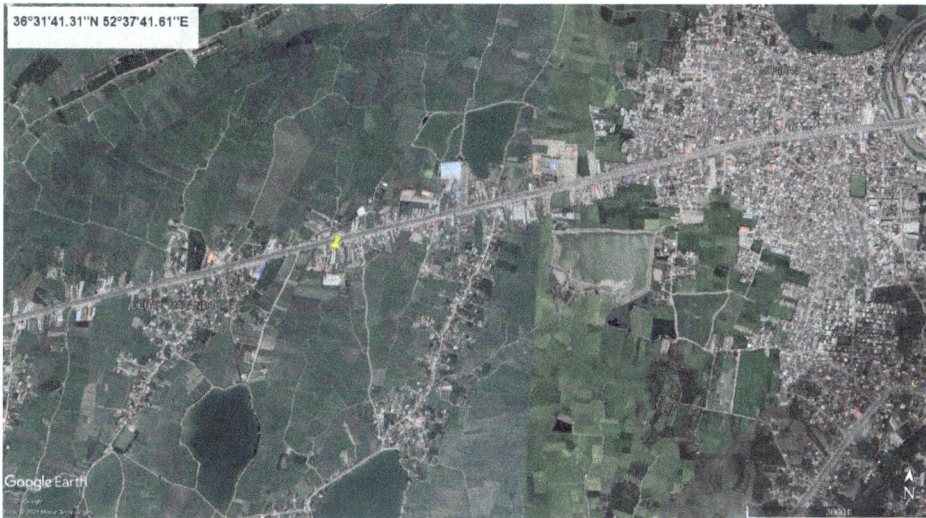

Basir Industries located at Km 1 of the Babol - Amol highway.

1.7. Bespar Sazeh Composite Company

Bespar Sazeh Composite manufactures UAV body parts. Established in 2015, the company primarily operates in the areas of design, modeling, molding and production of various composite and metal parts.

The original address of this company in 2015 was near the location of Quds Air Industries on Karaj Road. In 2016, it was moved to the Mallard area in the southwest of Tehran. The new location is near the IRGC missile and UAV barracks, including Falaq Barracks and Sajjad Barracks.

The managing director is Mohammad Reza Khosrojerdi, who is a close friend of Brigadier General Mohammad Baqer Qalibaf.

According to reports obtained from inside Iran, this company produces the fuselage of various types of UAVs, including for the so-called Mohajer drones. These reports indicate the company procures roughly 50% of its required raw materials from inside Iran. The remaining 50% is smuggled from abroad. At present, various types of raw materials are imported from China, Turkey and South Korea. In the past, the company imported high-quality glass fibers from France and some other materials, such as high-quality resin, from Germany and the United States. However, the regime is no longer able to do so as a result of sanctions, and instead obtains lower-quality raw materials from China.

The company's website states its products for the aviation industry include the "production of interior walls, wings, helicopter propellers, seats or interior decorations, among others." In addition, the company also produces composite material for the marine, oil and gas, petrochemical and construction industries.

The most recent information about some of the members of the company's board of directors is:

- Mohammad Reza Khosrojerdi (ID # 0057462453), CEO and chairman of the board
- Masoumeh Kakavand (ID # 0075777828), vice chairman of the board
- Mehdi Farshad, member of the board

Bespar Sazeh, involved in building Mohajer UAVs

1- Hall for production of composite parts; 2- Administrative office of Bespar Sazeh; 3- Office of Quds Air Industries

Picture taken from outside of Bespar Sazeh company

1.8. Ghazanfar Roknabadi Industries

Ghazanfar Roknabadi Industries, affiliated with the IRGC Aerospace Force, provides support and training for the IRGC Aerospace Force factories. It builds different parts of drones for the IRGC and other industries related to Aerospace.

This center is located at Old Karaj Road (Fatah Highway), Bilal Boulevard (Sepahe Islam), eastern side of the boulevard.

Ghazanfar Roknabadi complex located at Old Karaj Road (Fatah Highway)

The Ghazanfar Roknabadi complex includes dozens of sheds and buildings. The workspace for engines and drone cameras is located in the northern part of the complex.

The storage space for various parts related to the Aerospace Force is located in the southern part of the complex.

According to reports, the raw materials for the production of drone parts, such as fabrics and special fibers, are imported from China.

The center is named after the regime's former ambassador to Lebanon, who was killed during a Hajj pilgrimage in Saudi Arabia.

Ghazanfar Roknabadi Industries

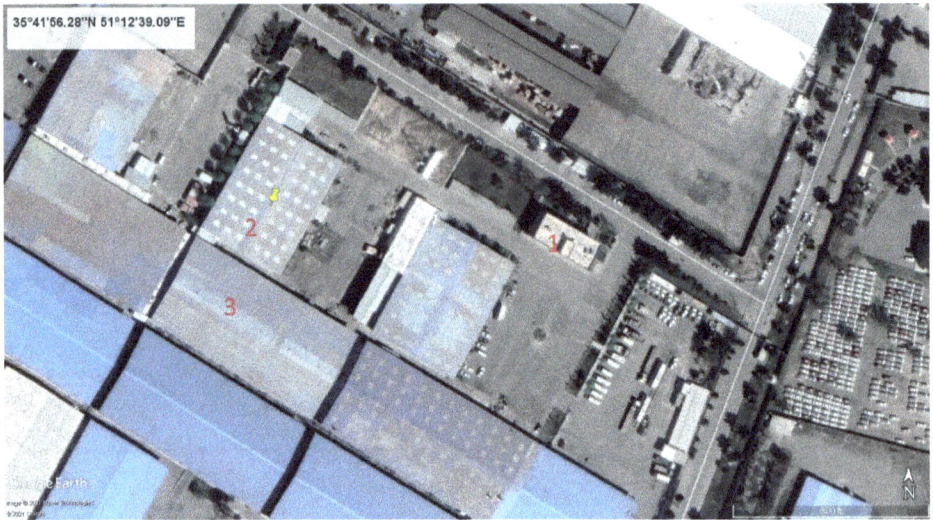

35°41'56.28"N 51°12'39.09"E

Bldg. 1- Security office; Bldg. 2- Engine and camera workshop;
Bldg. 3- Production Hall

1.9. Paravar Pars Company and Sepehr Airport

In 1995, the IRGC began setting up an airport and a military-industrial complex east of Imam Hossein University. The Sepehr Airport and the complex operate under the supervision of Paravar Pars Company, which belongs to the Aviation Research Unit of the IRGC's Imam Hossein University. The company copies existing models and builds UAVs, ultralight planes, and drones and also installs cameras and other equipment on drones. The Paravar Pars Company and Sepehr Airport have been placed under the control of the IRGC Aerospace Force since 2005, which uses the airport for training with drones and light aircraft.

The training facilities are controlled by the IRGC Bassij Commando Forces, the so-called Saberin Units. Many of IRGC forces who completed their training at this airport were sent to Syria, where many were killed.

The company's board of directors includes:

- Mohsen Asadi, CEO (outside members and partners)
- Alireza Tangsiri, chairman and member of the board
- Abolfazl Nazari, vice chairman and member of the board
- Abolfazl Salehnejad, member of the board
- Massoud Orei, member of the board

Sepehr Airport used by the IRGC for training with drones

- Abolghasem Valaghohar, member of the board
- Mohammad Reza Fadavi, member of the board
- Seyed Salman Seyed Afghahi, member of the board
- Sohrab Taghipour Ahangar, chief inspector
- Hossein Shamsabadi, alternate inspector

The current composition of the board of directors of Paravar Pars Company clearly shows the company's dependence on the IRGC. Alireza Tangsiri is the commander of the IRGC's Navy, Mohammad Reza Fadavi is a close relative of Ali Fadavi, deputy commander in chief of the IRGC, Mohsen Asadi and Seyed Salman Seyed Afghahi, both IRGC members, are officials of the Imam Hossein University.

Paravar Pars Co.

1.10. Armed Forces UAV Production Center in Semnan

Beginning in 2019, the regime's armed forces launched a new specialized drone unit headquartered in a complex in Semnan. All military institutions, including the IRGC, Bassij, State Security Forces (SSF) and Army defense, are jointly active in this complex, which is essentially a specialized working group for the production of UAVs, and works on the design and reproduction of light and quiet UAVs. A number of information technology specialists and engineers are working in this unit.

Drone production facility in Semnan

The drones produced are intended to control Iran's western and eastern borders. The specialists transport the parts in separate pieces to the desired locations and assemble the final products there. Their ultimate plan is to set up independent teams for each border province, where they can produce specific drones for the target area.

Other companies, such as Composite Structural Polymer, have been used by the IRGC in the cities of Karaj and Mashhad to produce other UAV parts.

1.11. Civilian companies used as covers for UAV part production

To provide the equipment and materials needed to build UAVs for terrorist purposes, the clerical regime is making extensive use of a network of companies it has established with civilian titles.

To that end, the "Iranian Aviation & Space Industries Association," has been formed which includes a group of seemingly civilian companies. The core of the association is made up of individuals such as Hamed Saeedi, Director of Farnas Pasargad, who are in contact with the IRGC and the Ministry of Defense.

In this manner, the Islamic Revolutionary Guard Corps uses these companies to purchase UAV accessories and equipment and circumvent sanctions. They make up a key smuggling ring of UAV parts and other aerospace industries' needs under the guise of civilian activities.

1. **Iranian Aviation & Space Industries Association.** Established in 2007, Iranian Aviation & Space Industries Association has been in close contact with the IRGC and the Ministry of Defense since its establishment, and most of its initial managers were in regular contact with the IRGC and the Ministry of Defense. On February 15, 2021, the last board of directors of the association was elected as follows: Soheil Soheili as the chairman, Amin Mehrabian as the first vice chairman, and Kambiz Khaghani as the second vice chairman. Also, Mostafa Sedighi was elected as treasurer, and Reza Aslani, Masoud Ghasemi and Seyed Yaser Mohseni Zonouzi were elected as members of the board of

directors for three years. Bahman Eftekhar Fard Nazari was elected as the chief inspector for one year. Since 2019, Massoud Ghasemi, who is the nephew of IRGC Brig. General Saeed Ghasemi, has been the chairman. Massoud Ghasemi is also a member of the Alborz Province Chamber of Commerce and uses this chamber to circumvent sanctions.

Massoud Ghasemi, Member, Board of Directors, Iranian Aviation & Space Industries Association

2. **Iranian Aviation & Space Industries Working Group.** One of the most important sub-groups of the Iranian Aviation & Space Industries Association is Iranian Aviation & Space Industries Working

From left: Hamed Saeedi, a key figure of the UAV working group; Saeed Aghajani, UAV commander of the IRGC Aerospace Force

Group. The key person is Hamed Saeedi, who also chaired the board of directors of the group for several years. Saeedi has close ties with Saeed Aghajani, UAV commander of the IRGC Aerospace Force. He is also associated with Quds Aerospace Industries (the main manufacturer of UAVs for the Ministry of Defense). On July 10, 2021, Mohsen Siadatnejad was appointed head of the aerospace industry UAV working group.

3. **Iranian Research Organization for Science and Technology (IROST).** IROST is related to the regime's Ministry of Science, which works on scientific research projects, such as the aerospace and UAV industries. This organization has close ties with the clerical regime's Ministry of Defense. Using the cover of a civilian organization, it supplies a portion of the parts and equipment by circumventing sanctions. The organization is located in the Ahmadabad Mostofi Asr-e-Enghelab Research Complex. Address: Tehran — Azadegan Highway — North to South route — Ahmadabad Mostofi — after Parsa Square — end of Enghelab Street — Shahid Ehsani Rad Street.

Iranian Research Organization for Science and Technology (IROST) located in Tehran.

4. **Iravin Innovation and Acceleration Center.** This center was established as a research center in 2021. The company is a knowledge-based (research) company that works on various technologies, such as UAV, satellite, rail, and sea transport. Hamed Saeedi is one of the main managers of this center as well.

5. **Farnas Pasargad Aerospace Industries Company.** Hamed Saeedi, CEO of Farnas Pasargad Aerospace Industries Company, has had joint projects with the Armed Forces and especially with the IRGC, in addition to building spy drones. The company states: "Farnas Pasargad Aerospace Industries has been working in the field of aerospace engineering, electronics, telecommunications, parts manufacturing, etc. since 1999 as a semi-public sector and as a private and registered company since 2005. It has provided high-tech projects and products to various government industries, the armed forces, and the country's industrial and academic complexes."

It is located in Neka Industrial Town, Phase 1, in the Mazandaran province.

Hamed Saeedi (left) shows how to navigate a drone to the regime's Supreme Leader, Ali Khamenei (center).

6. **Bal Gostar Negah Asemanha Technology.** Manufactures UAV parts in cooperation with the regime's military aerospace industry. Its head is Mohammad Chitgarha. The company was established on December 27, 2016. Chitgarha participated in the filming of the demonstrations in 2017 and cooperates with the clerical regime's radio and television network.

7. **Kharazmi Electronics Industries.** It was established in 2001. Hossein Tavangar, ID# 0058486275, is the CEO of Kharazmi Electronics Industries. He uses the front company to circumvent sanctions to procure supplies of electronic components for aircraft, helicopters, electronic missile boards and UAVs.

8. **Iran Bekr Part Khavar Mianeh.** Ali Asghar Jafari is the CEO of the company, established on May 11, 2009, and works in the field of helicopter parts, aircraft, UAVs, missiles, electronics and avionics, telecommunications, radar, and electronic countermeasure, while circumventing sanctions.

9. **Sahfa Production-Distribution Cooperative Company – Iranian Aerospace Industries.** The company is a subset of the Iranian Aviation & Space Industries Association. One of the main managers, Amir Reza Naderi, ID# 0045159726, for several years has been a member of the board of directors of the Iranian Aerospace Industries Association. He has been the executive director of international exhibitions of the aerospace industries in Tehran as well. He is a member of the board of directors of Pars Aviation Development Investment, Negin Asia Map, Aroko Pouye Persia and several other companies.

10. **Aras Tech Aircraft Maintenance Services Company.** The company participates in the supply of parts for the aerospace and UAV industries by circumventing sanctions. Its chairman, Bahman Eftekhar Fard Nazari, has previously been a member the Aerospace Industry board of directors.

11. **Maham Pergas Technology.** Established on April 15, 2017. The chairman of the board of directors is IRGC General (pilot) Mohammad Norouzi, ID# 0047666501, whose job is to purchase equipment,

including parts, aircraft, and related training. Norouzi is notorious for abusing his positions in military establishments for theft and embezzlement.

12. **Hezareh Sevvom Industrial Alloy Development Company.** The company supplies metals and other materials for the Ministry of Defense and the Atomic Energy Organization. Ali Ghorban Shiroodi, vice chairman of the board of directors, ID# 045256735, is also a member of the board of directors at Moaser Alloy Trade Development and Kosar Health Supply.

13. **Nazari Titanium Company.** The company imports metal materials, especially titanium, and it is controlled by two brothers, Mehdi and Bahman Nazari. The company works on behalf of the Ministry of Defense, the Ministry of Oil, the Atomic Energy Organization, among others, procuring and supplying embargoed items by circumventing sanctions using interest and mafia networks inside and outside the country. It has offices in Turkey, UAE, and Hong Kong.

14. **Sara Safe Tools.** Imports aircraft and aviation equipment and is active in circumventing sanctions. Mohsen Shakiba is the CEO, ID# 0055985025.

15. **Noandishan Composite Structures Industrial-Production.** As one of the companies of the Iran Aerospace Industries Association, it works on the production of composite parts (fiberglass). Its board members are Ali Makhmali and Ali Gholami.

1.12. Procurement of UAV parts smuggled from abroad

According to reports obtained from inside the IRGC, despite the public propaganda that UAVs are made locally by the regime, Tehran procures various UAV parts through smuggling from outside Iran. Under the guise of this enterprise, the IRGC engages in astronomical financial theft.

One of the concerns of companies affiliated with the IRGC in purchasing parts from outside Iran is whether the imported equipment might have destructive devices embedded in it. Therefore, they try to keep the information about their purchases from abroad secret to reduce the probability of sabotage.

1.13. Specs on some of the drones produced by the IRGC

Ababil UAV: This small UAV was designed roughly in the middle of the Iran-Iraq War in 1986. Its production was launched by HESA (Iran Aircraft Manufacturing Company). It has a piston engine and can be launched from a metal rail that can be mounted on a pickup truck with the help of a rocket booster, and landed with an parachute. This drone is used for kamikaze attacks. The regime has provided this type of drone to Hezbollah and Hamas.

Ababil UAV was designed in the middle of the Iran-Iraq War in 1986. Tehran has provided these UAVs, which is used for kamikaze attacks, to Hezbollah and Hamas.

Mojaher-4 UAV: This UAV was built in the early 2000s. The older models were called the Immigrant 1, 2, and 3. The drone is equipped with two small air-to-air missiles called *Misagh*. Mohajer-4 has no wheels and is fired from metal rails. It is manufactured by the Quds Air Industries. The engine and radar equipment are smuggled from abroad, particularly from Germany, while the rest of the parts are made in Iran. Newer types of this UAV, called Mohajer-6, have been produced in subsequent years.

Mohajer-4 drone

Shahed-129 UAV: The Shahed-129 drone is considered to be the main combat reconnaissance drone for the regime. This drone is similar to the American-made MQ1 combat drone. It has been on the regime's production line since 2013 and its range is about 1,700 km. These drones have been targeted and shot down several times by the US Air Force in Syria.

Shahed-129 unmanned aerial vehicle (UAV) loaded with Sadid missiles

Shahed-129 UAV of the Iranian regime crashed near the Iranian border in Pakistan

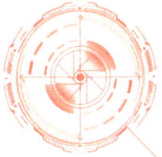

2.
UTILIZATION OF UAVS

2.1. History of the IRGC's use of UAVs

In 1985, in the course of the Iran-Iraq War, the IRGC created, along with the formation of the Hadid missile unit, the Raad UAV unit for the use of drones in the war. This unit later turned into a battalion and a brigade within the IRGC Air Force. The IRGC Air Force later became the Aerospace Force, and this brigade was turned into the UAV Command.

Currently, UAVs are used in various forces of the IRGC, the Army and the State Security Forces (SSF), but the main organ that uses UAVs is called the UAV Command, which is a subset of the IRGC Aerospace Force.

2.2. UAV Command of the IRGC Aerospace Force

The UAV Command Center is one of the IRGC Aerospace's subsidiaries. In addition to UAV Command, the IRGC Aerospace Force has a Missile Command, Air Command, Air Defense Command, and Space Command, among others.

```
┌─────────────────────────────────────────────────────────┐
│       UAV Command in the Aerospace Force of the IRGC      │
└─────────────────────────────────────────────────────────┘

                    ┌──────────────────────┐
                    │  IRGC Aerospace Force │
                    └──────────────────────┘
```

| Space Command | Air Command | UAV Command | Air Defense Command | Missile Command |

| Ahvaz UAV Unit | Kermanshah UAV Unit | Isfahan UAV Unit | Kashan UAV Unit |

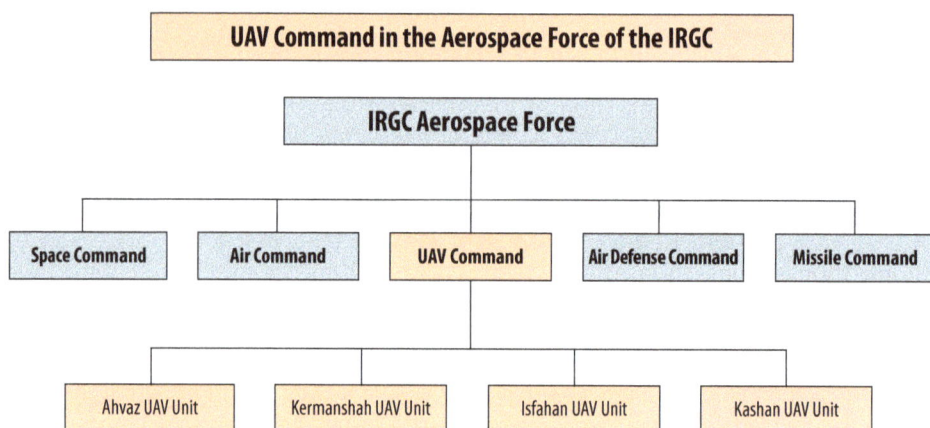

The IRGC Aerospace Force UAV Command Center has locations in different parts of Iran. Its headquarters is located in a section of the Dastvareh Barracks (headquarters of the IRGC Aerospace Force) in the northwest of Tehran. Units in other cities include Kashan, Ahvaz, Kermanshah and Isfahan.

2.2.1. Location of IRGC Aerospace UAV Command (Dastvareh Barracks)

The UAV Command Center is located in the Dastvareh Barracks, which is also the headquarters of the IRGC Aerospace Force. The Command Center is housed in a separate building. Brig. Gen. Saeed Aqajani (Aghajani), the current commander of the IRGC Aerospace Force UAV Command, works out of this area.

2.2.2. Kashan UAV unit — Karimi Base

The Karimi Air Base is one of the largest locations for the drone units of the IRGC Aerospace Force. It is adjacent to Kashan Airport. Some of the IRGC's drones are stored there. This base is used to train foreign mercenaries. Some of the unit's personnel were sent to Syria, where they were killed at T4 Airport near the Syrian city of Palmyra. Among them was Mehdi

UAV command is located at Dastvareh Garrison, which is IRGC's Aerospace Force headquarters.

Entrance of Dastvareh Garrison

Dehqan Yazdeli, who was in charge of the command office of Karimi Air Base from 2004 until his death in Syria. The current commander of the Karimi Base is Colonel Morteza Farmanian. His designated successor was Sanatkar, whose official title was political deputy and was dispatched to Syria on March 14, 2018 and killed on April 9, 2018.

The Karimi Air Base, one of the largest locations for the drone units of the IRGC Aerospace Force, is adjacent to Kashan Airport.

2.2.3. Isfahan UAV unit — Badr Base

This IRGC Aerospace Force Base is one of the centers of UAV units. Located in the south of the city of Isfahan, the base provides training on the use of UAVs.

Badr Base of IRGC Aerospace Force is located in the south of the city of Isfahan, and provides training on the use of UAVs.

2.2.4. Ahvaz UAV unit

An IRGC drone unit is located in Ahvaz. This unit has also sent some of its personnel to Syria. One of them, Seyyed Ammar Moussavi Moshasha'e, was a member of the Aerospace Force UAV unit in Ahvaz. He was killed on April 9, 2018, at T-4 Airport near the Syrian city of Palmyra. Prior to his death, he had carried out many missions in Iraq and Syria. Ammar Moussavi was killed along with six others in an attack on the headquarters of the IRGC drone unit at Syria's T4 airport.

2.2.5. Kermanshah UAV unit

Another UAV unit of the IRGC Aerospace Force is located near the city of Kermanshah. Some of the unit's personnel are sent by the Quds Force on missions in the region.

2.2.6. Sajjad Barracks

The Sajjad Barracks of the IRGC Aerospace Force is located in the Mallard area (west of Tehran). It belongs to the IRGC's 19th Zulfaqar missile group and has for a long time served as one of the storage sites for IRGC Naze'at missiles and UAVs. Due to the importance of this site, the IRGC has installed air defense systems around it.

Sajjad Barracks of the IRGC Aerospace Force located in the Mallard area (west of Tehran).

2.2.7. Falaq Barracks

The Falaq Barracks of the IRGC Aerospace Forces is located in the Mallard region. It hosts some of the logistics and research activities of the IRGC Aerospace Force. A portion of warehouse spaces in the barracks is dedicated to the storage of UAVs and their parts.

35°33'45.45"N 50°53'57.43"E

Falaq Barracks of the IRGC Aerospace Forces located in the Mallard region hosts some of the logistics and research activities of the IRGC Aerospace Force. A portion of the barracks is used for storage of UAVs and their parts.

2.3. UAV Command of IRGC Ground Forces

Currently, the UAV Commander in the IRGC Ground Forces is Brigadier General Karim Akbarloo. Previously, Akbarloo worked in the technical department of the IRGC's intelligence organization. He travels to China in order to procure more advanced equipment. The IRGC Ground Forces UAV unit primarily uses small tactical UAVs, some of which are launched manually and do not require a platform. These drones are provided to IRGC Ground Forces brigades and are used for limited reconnaissance and artillery attacks. Larger drones are kept by the IRGC Aerospace Force, and are assigned to the Ground Forces for missions.

2.4. Use of UAVs by other IRGC and Army forces

The regime also uses UAVs for both reconnaissance and operational plans by the IRGC Navy, the Army's three forces, and the SSF.

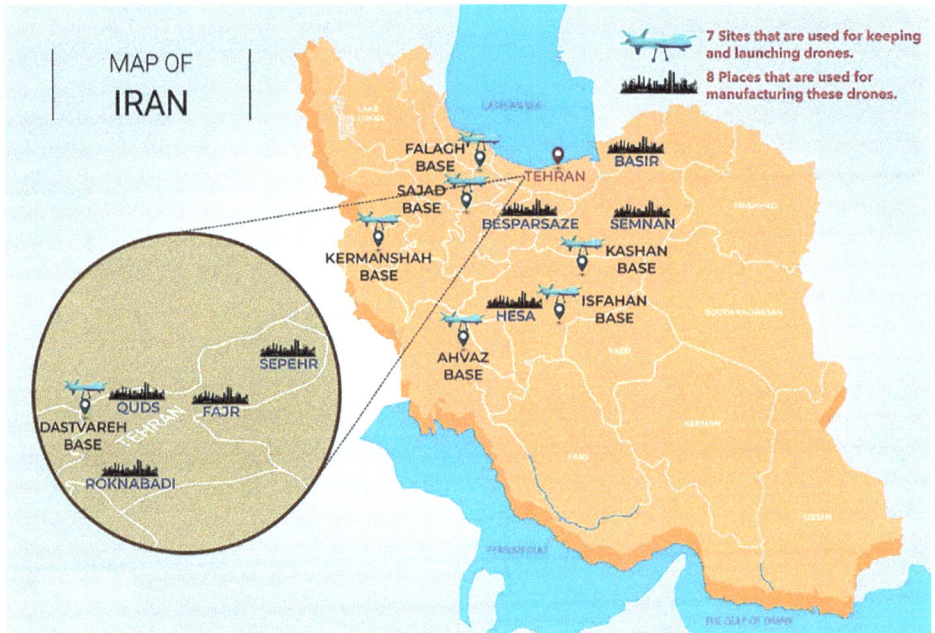

MAP OF
IRAN

7 Sites that are used for keeping and launching drones.

8 Places that are used for manufacturing these drones.

FALAGH BASE

BASIR

SAJAD BASE

TEHRAN

BESPARSAZE

SEMNAN

KERMANSHAH BASE

KASHAN BASE

HESA

ISFAHAN BASE

SEPEHR

AHVAZ BASE

QUDS

FAJR

DASTVAREH BASE

ROKNABADI

Locations of 8 sites used for manufacturing and 7 sites used for keeping and launching UAVs

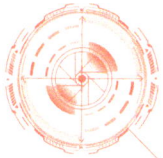

3.
USING UAVS TO INCITE WAR AND TERRORISM

The IRGC's Quds Force systematically trains its mercenary groups in the region to use and build UAVs. The IRGC Air Force UAV Command sends its specialists to Iraq, Syria, Lebanon, Yemen, and Palestine to train locals in the utilization of UAVs.

3.1. Quds Force Intelligence

A management subdivision of the Quds Force Intelligence Directorate orders the manufacture of various munitions, including drones, missiles, and other weapons required by the Quds Force to intervene in other countries. This department is related to the Aerospace Industry, the Aviation Industries Organization and the Defense Industry Organization, the organs manufacturing various weapons in the Ministry of Defense. At the time of the Coalition's presence in Iraq, Quds Force Intelligence ordered the construction of drones as well as anti-aircraft missiles to be sent to Iraq.

3.2. Quds Force Training

In addition to training in the use of missiles, the Quds Force of the IRGC has systematically placed UAV training in the orders of the Deputy for Training (code 12000).

There are different training groups in Imam Ali Garrison (located at 20 km of Tehran-Karaj highway), which is the training center of the Quds Force. One of the groups is the so-called "specialized" (technical) unit. This group includes three subdivisions: UAV, missiles, and heavy weaponry and its repair. The specialized training unit is commanded by IRGC Colonel Ali Mohammad. The missile training section is known as code 340. UAV training is code 330. Heavy weapons and repairs is code 320.

In addition to providing training on the use of missiles, the specialized unit of the Training Department, which is located near the city of Semnan, provides training on the use of drones to the mercenaries of the Quds Force.

Some areas of higher-level training on the use of UAVs are provided by UAV experts of the IRGC Aerospace Force at the Karimi Base in Kashan.

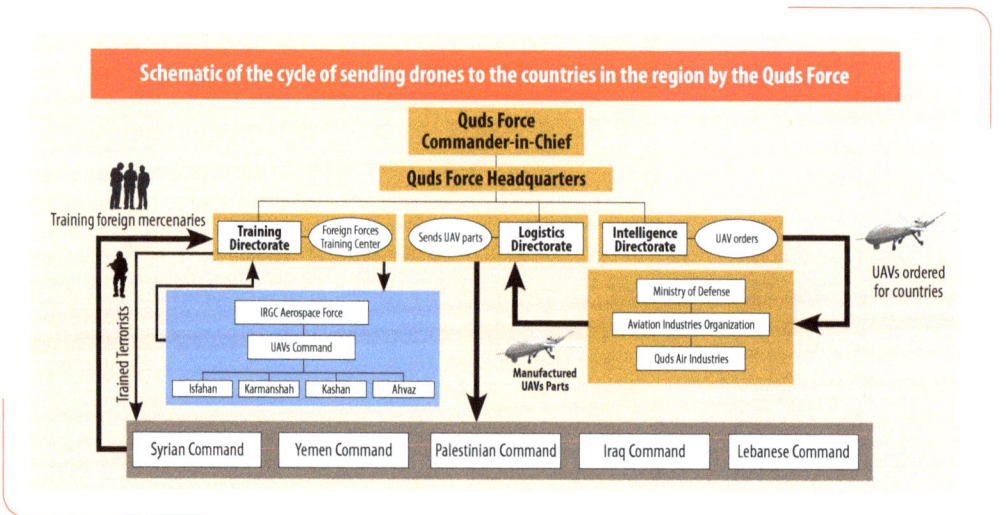

Schematic of the cycle of sending drones to the countries in the region by the Quds Force

3.3. Quds Force Logistics and Support

Within this Quds Force Logistics and Support Directorate, a division (referred to as Unit 190) is responsible for arms and equipment smuggling to the countries of the region. This office uses various air, land and sea pathways to send weapons and equipment, including UAV parts. In this way, the Quds Force, in conjunction with the Ministry of Defense and the Aerospace Force, transfers UAV weapons, training and other requirements to its mercenary groups.

> **Air:** Some of the weapons and equipment are routinely sent to target countries through the IRGC base at Mehrabad Airport.

> **Land:** Some of this equipment, hidden in containers, is sent overland by truck to Iraq, Syria and Lebanon.

> **Sea:** Other equipment is smuggled on IRGC boats through ports controlled by the IRGC to Yemen and other areas.

Quds Force uses various air, land and sea pathways to send weapons and equipment, including UAV parts to its proxies in the region.

3.4. UAV attack on Saudi oil refinery

One of the most important terrorist operations carried out by the IRGC Aerospace Force using both drones and missiles was the attack on the Aramco oil refinery in 2019. The general plan of operation was decided on Wednesday, July 31, 2019, during a special meeting of the regime's Supreme National Security Council. According to specific information, some of the commanders of the IRGC who participated in this meeting were: General Gholam Ali Rashid, Commander of Khatam al-Anbia Central Command (the highest-ranking military operations base in Iran, responsible for planning and operational coordination of the regime's armed forces, including the IRGC and the Army); Maj. Gen. Hossein Salami, Commander-in-Chief of the IRGC; Maj. Gen. Qassem Soleimani, Commander of the Quds Force; and Brigadier General Amir Ali Hajizadeh, Commander of the IRGC Aerospace Force. Rashid and Hajizadeh were attending this meeting of the Supreme National Security Council to discuss this specific operation. In addition to these individuals, several army commanders also attended.

After carrying out the planning for various parts of the operation and making the final decision on the implementation, the plan was sent to Khamenei for final approval. Khamenei, as the regime's commander-in-chief, ordered General Rashid and Brigadier General Hajizadeh to execute the operation.

About a week before the missile attack, the team of commanders of this operation left the IRGC Aerospace Force headquarters and traveled to Khuzestan Province in southwestern Iran. Some of the commanders in this team who have been identified include Brigadier General Mohammad Fallah, Deputy Chief of Aerospace Operations; Brigadier General Mahmoud Bagheri Kazemabad, Commander of the Missile Unit of the Aerospace Force; and Brigadier General Saeed Aqajani (Aghajani), Commander of the Drone Unit of the Aerospace Force.

This command team was stationed in a section of Omidiyeh Base, in the area between Omidiyeh and Ahvaz in Khuzestan, about 85 km from Ahvaz. The Omidiyeh base, formerly the Army Air Force's fifth fighter jet base, served as the headquarters of the Tactical Operations Command.

The Omidiyeh base, formerly the Army Air Force's fifth fighter jet base, served as the headquarters of the Tactical Operations Command for UAV attack on Saudi oil refinery in September 2019.

3.5. Sending drones to Syria

The IRGC Aerospace Force drone unit was one of the first IRGC units to enter Syria in the beginning of the Syrian conflict in 2011–2012, and has played an active role in providing assistance to the Syrian army in its fight against opposition forces. The commanders of the IRGC drone unit were stationed at various command centers, including the cities of Palmyra (T4 Airport), Damascus (Al-Mazza Airport), Deir ez-Zor and Al-Bukamal. They used different types of drones in Syria, some of which have been shot down, including the Shahed-129 drone.

A number of IRGC Aerospace Force personnel are currently stationed in Syria (as of the summer of 2021). One of the airports used to operate UAVs is the Palmyra Airport, where IRGC Aerospace Force guards are stationed and conduct operations. The headquarters of the IRGC Aerospace Force is in the city of Palmyra.

The drones sent to Syria are sent in pieces, and when they arrive, the IRGC assembles them in its workshops and factories. Parts such as UAV engines are purchased directly from China and shipped to Syria.

3.6. Sending drones to Iraq

The IRGC's Quds Force has been sending drones to Iraq for IRGC-affiliated militias since the arrival of Coalition forces in Iraq. In the years since the withdrawal of the multi-national forces, the IRGC has made extensive use of drones inside Iraq, making them available to IRGC-affiliated militant groups. In a parade organized by the Popular Mobilization Front in June 2021, these groups, including Al-Nujaba, displayed their drones. All the parts of these drones had been sent by the IRGC from Iran.

The parts are shipped individually to Baghdad Airport or by land, for use by the Hashad al-Shaabi groups. These parts are assembled in IRGC-affiliated workshops, one of which is located at Ashraf Garrison. At present, this garrison is basically under the control of the Badr group. But it is also used by Kataib Hezbollah and Asaeb Ahl-e-Haq.

Iraqi mercenary groups of the Quds Force use kamikaze drones to carry out large-scale attacks on international coalition forces based in Iraq,

One of the Mohajer-6 UAVs delivered by the Iranian regime to Al-Nujaba group in Iraq, one of the mercenary groups of the Quds Force, on display during a parade organized by the Popular Mobilization Front in June 2021.

A Quds Yasir UAV produced by the Iranian regime provided to Al-Nujaba group tied to the Quds Force of the IRGC

which have killed and wounded coalition forces and civilian contractors. For example, an attack took place at Erbil Airport on February 15, 2021, in which a US civilian contractor was killed immediately. Another individual among the five wounded died a few days later.[15] Other attacks include Erbil Airport, the base of the international coalition forces, on April 14, 2021[16]; two drone attacks against the Ayn al Asad Base on June 6, 2021[17]; an attack against the American base in Erbil on June 26, 2021[18]; and an attack on American forces in Erbil Airport on September 12, 2021.[19]

15   John Davison, Ahmed Rasheed, "U.S. forces in Iraq hit by rockets, contractor killed." *Reuters*, February 15, 2021, https://www.reuters.com/article/us-iraq-security/u-s-forces-in-iraq-hit-by-rockets-contractor-killed-idUSKBN2AF1SH.

16   "Explosives-laden drone targets U.S. forces at Iraq's Erbil airport," *Reuters*, April 14, 2021, https://www.reuters.com/world/middle-east/rocket-hits-near-erbil-airport-northern-iraq-kurdish-security-officials-2021-04-14.

17   "Two drones intercepted, shot down over Iraqi air base — military," *Reuters*, June 6, 2021, https://www.reuters.com/world/middle-east/two-drones-intercepted-shot-down-over-iraqi-air-base-military-2021-06-06.

18   "Drones hit near Iraq's Erbil," *The Jordan Times*, November 29, 2021, https://www.jordantimes.com/news/region/drones-hit-near%C2%A0iraqs-erbil.

19   "Drone attack hits near US forces stationed at Erbil airport in northern Iraq," *France 24*, December 9, 2021, https://www.france24.com/en/middle-east/20210912-drone-attack-hits-near-us-forces-stationed-at-erbil-airport-in-northern-iraq.

3.7. Sending drones to Lebanon

In 2003, seven members of the Lebanese Hezbollah received training for the first time on the Mohajer-4 aircraft at the Quds Air Industries, which produces UAVs. Subsequently, the regime sent several of these aircraft to Hezbollah in Lebanon. Due to the importance of using UAVs for terrorist acts, in 2006, Imad Mughniyeh, using the pseudonym "Haj Mohsen," secretly went to Tehran and visited Sepehr Airport (along with 2-3 others) to see how UAVs were launched from vehicles. According to reports, the UAVs he inspected were 6 to 9 feet long. The head of the Paravar Pars Company at the time received a two-million-dollar contract from the Iranian regime to produce UAVs to arm Hezbollah.

3.8. Sending drones to Yemen

The IRGC's Quds Force also provides drones to the Yemeni Ansarollah (Houthis) on a wide scale. The Houthis consistently use drones in their attacks, and their drones are constantly shot down in Saudi territory. According to a report on November 27, 2016, the seizure of six Qasef-1 UAVs being transferred from Oman to Yemen (a common smuggling route) shows that the Qasef-1 was not made in Yemen but transferred from Iran.[20] The Qasef-1 drone is similar to the Ababil-2 drones built by the IRGC.

The Yemeni National Army announced on April 4th, 2019, that it had shot down an Iranian-made Ababil T UAV belonging to Houthi militants before it had reached its target in the Al-Faza area in western Al-Hudaidah Province.[21]

Earlier, a UN special committee of experts identified foreign components of the downed drones as Iranian-made.[22] The Houthis, with the help of

---

20 "Maritime Interdictions of Weapon Supplies to Somalia and Yemen: Deciphering a link to Iran," Conflict Armament Research Ltd., 2016, https://www.conflictarm.com/dispatches/maritime-interdictions-of-weapon-supplies-to-somalia-and-yemen.

21 "Yemeni army shot down an Iranian-made Houthi drone in al-Hudaidah," *Al-Arabiya Farsi,* April 4, 2021, https://bit.ly/3xsfF0t

22 "Letter dated 25 January 2019 from the Panel of Experts on Yemen addressed to the President of the Security Council," *United Nations Security Council,* January 25, 2019, https://www.securitycouncilreport.org/atf/cf/%7B65BFCF9B-6D27-4E9C-8CD3-CF6E4FF96FF9%7D/s_2019_83.pdf.

A Qasef UAV produced by the Iranian regime and used by the Yemeni Ansarollah

Iranian military experts, assemble the components in Sanaa and other areas under their control and then launch them into Saudi Arabia and other areas controlled by the Yemeni National Army.[23]

A downed UAV of the Iranian regime in west of Al Hadidah in Yemen

---

23 Damien McElroy, "Germany stops Iran buying mini-engines after they were found in Houthi drones," *The National News,* September 24, 2020, https://www.thenationalnews.com/world/germany-stops-iran-buying-mini-engines-after-they-were-found-in-houthi-drones-1.1083080.

The senior commander of the Quds Force in Yemen is an international terrorist named Abdul Reza Shahlai. He was first designated by the U.S. Treasury Department in 2008 for his activities in Iraq and was further designated as terrorist under E.O. 13224 as a Specially Designated Global Terrorist in 2011.

Abdul Reza Shahlai, Senior Quds Force commander in Yemen

3.9. Sending drones to Palestine

The IRGC's Quds Force has a special unit called the Palestine Affairs Office, which meddles in Palestinian affairs. The Quds Force conducts a large-scale operation, sending drones to Islamic Jihad and Hamas groups in Palestine to incite war and terrorism in the region. Brigadier General Mohammad Saeed Izadi, who is often based in Lebanon, is in charge of Palestinian affairs in the Quds Force.

3.10. Attacks in Kurdish regions

The clerical regime also uses drones to attack the Kurdish regions in order to suppress Iranian Kurdish groups and refugees.[24]

---

24   Dilan Sirwan, "KDPI claims to have downed 4 of 16 drones used by Iran in Kurdistan Region," *Rudaw,* September 13, 2021, https://www.rudaw.net/english/kurdistan/130920213.

4.
CONCLUSION

A review of the cycle of production, use and export of drones and its expansion in recent years reveals the following:

1. Despite and in part due to the concessions made through the nuclear deal and Western countries' decision to turn a blind eye to the clerical regime's destabilizing activities, the export of terrorism and incitement to war in the region remain a pillar for the regime's preservation, and have gained more prominence in the eyes of the ruling clerics.

2. Since the installation of Ebrahim Raisi as the Iranian regime's president by Supreme Leader Ali Khamenei, the destructive intervention of the Quds Force in the region has intensified, as have Tehran's UAV attacks.

3. The regime is spending billions of dollars on its missiles and UAV programs, while 80 percent of the Iranian people live below the poverty line and the budgets for health care, education and other national requirements are abysmally lower than military expenditures. During the coronavirus pandemic, the regime did not assist the Iranian people in any way; the number of victims has surpassed 490,000 to date, by far outpacing other countries on a per capita basis. Over the past few years, the Iranian people have chanted, "No to Gaza, no to Lebanon, my life only for Iran," and "Leave Syria, think about us instead."

4. These activities prove that the billions of dollars that the regime received from the easing of sanctions in the context of the

nuclear deal and plundered from Iran's national wealth have been expropriated to build and produce weapons in order to export regional terrorism and warmongering.

5. Any dealings with the regime in Tehran by all Western sides, especially after the ascendance of Raisi, must end. All activities relevant to the production, use and research of drones and the regime's missile program, must be included in any list of demands. Otherwise, because of its severe domestic weakness, the clerical regime will place more emphasis on creating regional instability in order to buy time and preserve its rule.

6. None of the sanctions against the regime should be lifted until it has stopped all its rogue behavior and its repression of the Iranian people.

5. LIST OF PUBLICATIONS

List of Publications by the National Council of Resistance of Iran, U.S. Representative Office

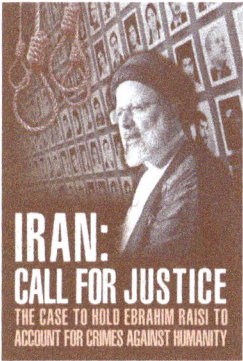

IRAN: Call for Justice

The Case to Hold Ebrahim Raisi to Account for Crimes Against Humanity

September 2021, 108 pages

This manuscript makes the case for bringing the clerical regime's president Ebrahim Raisi to justice before an international tribunal for the 1988 massacre, a clear case of crimes against humanity.

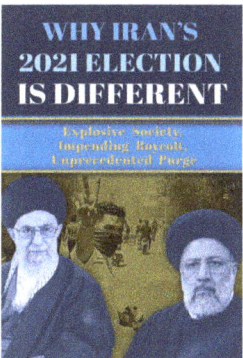

Why Iran's 2021 Election Is Different:

Explosive Society, Impending Boycott, Unprecedented Purge

May 2021, 80 pages

This report highlights the difference between the 2021 election and all prior 12 presidential elections in Iran.

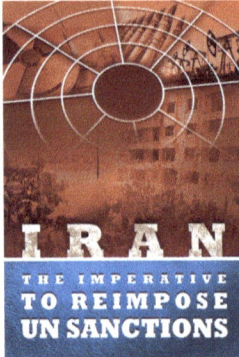

IRAN - The Imperative to Reimpose UN Sanctions

August 2020, 108 pages

This report shows how the Iranian regime is involved in procuring and manufacturing weapons and military equipment with the objective of exporting terrorism and warmongering, regional meddling by sending weapons and missiles to expand terrorist attacks, and resorts to terrorism.

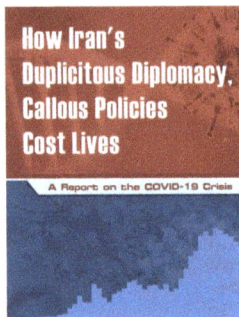

How Iran's Duplicitous Diplomacy, Callous Policies Cost Lives

A Report on the COVID-19 Crisis

April 2020, 84 pages

This report seeks to show that the Iranian Foreign Ministry's campaign to lift sanctions is replete with lies and misleading claims, with the goal of cynically exploiting the coronavirus pandemic to the regime's benefit In effect, the mullahs are causing the death of thousands of Iranians to preserve their own rule.

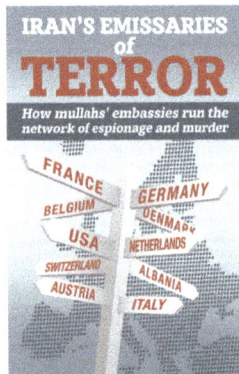

Iran's Emissaries of Terror

June 2019, 208 pages

This book explains the extent to which Tehran's embassies and diplomats are at the core of both the planning and execution of international terrorism targeting Iranian dissidents, as well as central to Tehran's direct and proxy terrorism against other countries.

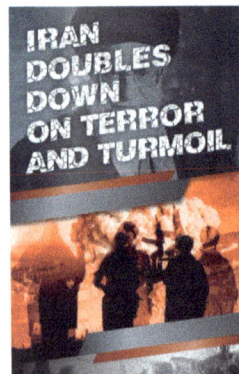

Iran Doubles Down on Terror and Turmoil

November 2018, 63 pages

This book examines the regime's political and economic strategy, which revolves around terrorism and physical annihilation of opponents. Failing to quell growing popular protests, Tehran has bolstered domestic suppression with blatant terrorism and intimidation.

Iran Will Be Free:
Speech by Maryam Rajavi
September 2018, 54 pages

Text of a keynote speech delivered by Mrs. Maryam Rajavi on June 30, 2018, at the Iranian Resistance's grand gathering in Paris, France explaining the path to freedom in Iran and what she envisions for future Iran.

Iran's Ballistic Buildup:
The March Toward Nuclear-Capable Missiles
May 2018, 136 pages

This manuscript surveys Iran's missile capabilities, including the underlying organization, structure, production, and development infrastructure, as well as launch facilities and the command centers. The book exposes the nexus between the regime's missile activities and its nuclear weapons program, including ties with North Korea.

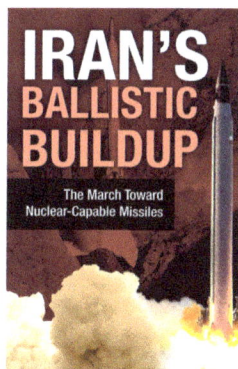

Iran: Cyber Repression: How the IRGC Uses Cyberwarfare to Preserve the Theocracy
February 2018, 70 pages

This manuscript demonstrates how the Iranian regime, under the supervision and guidance of the IRGC and the Ministry of Intelligence and Security (MOIS), have employed new cyberwarfare and tactics in a desperate attempt to counter the growing dissent inside the country.

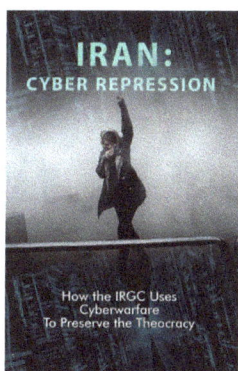

Iran: Where Mass Murderers Rule: The 1988 Massacre of 30,000 Political Prisoners and the Continuing Atrocities
November 2017, 161 pages

Iran: Where Mass Murderers Rule is an expose of the current rulers of Iran and their track record in human rights violations. The book details how 30,000 political prisoners fell victim to politicide during the summer of 1988 and showcases the egregious political extinction of a group of people.

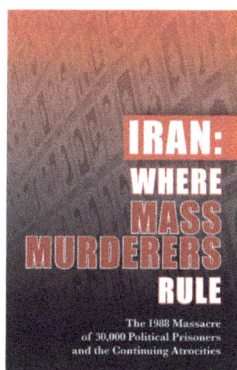

Iran's Nuclear Core: Uninspected Military Sites, Vital to the Nuclear Weapons Program

October 2017, 52 pages

This book details how the nuclear weapons program is at the heart of, and not parallel to, the civil nuclear program of Iran. The program has been run by the Islamic Revolutionary Guards Corp (IRGC) since the beginning, and the main nuclear sites and nuclear research facilities have been hidden from the eyes of the United Nations nuclear watchdog.

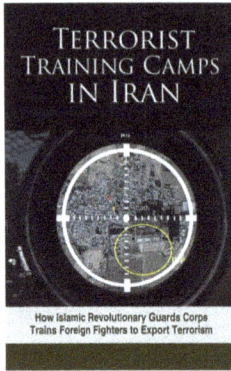

Terrorist Training Camps in Iran: How Islamic Revolutionary Guards Corps Trains Foreign Fighters to Export Terrorism

June 2017, 56 pages

The book details how Islamic Revolutionary Guards Corps trains foreign fighters in 15 various camps in Iran to export terrorism. The IRGC has created a large directorate within its extraterritorial arm, the Quds Force, in order to expand its training of foreign mercenaries as part of the strategy to step up its meddling abroad in Syria, Iraq, Yemen, Bahrain, Afghanistan and elsewhere.

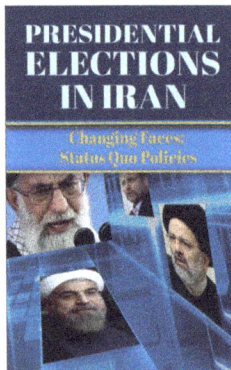

Presidential Elections in Iran: Changing Faces; Status Quo Policies

May 2017, 78 pages

The book reviews the past 11 presidential elections, demonstrating that the only criterion for qualifying as a candidate is practical and heartfelt allegiance to the Supreme Leader. An unelected vetting watchdog, the Guardian Council makes that determination.

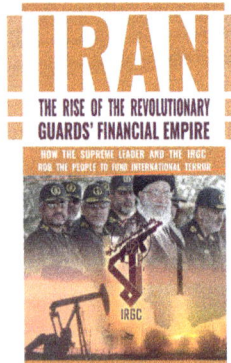

The Rise of Iran's Revolutionary Guards' Financial Empire: How the Supreme Leader and the IRGC Rob the People to Fund International Terror

March 2017, 174 pages

This study shows how ownership of property in various spheres of the economy is gradually shifted from the population writ large towards a minority ruling elite comprised of the Supreme Leader's office and the IRGC, using 14 powerhouses, and how the money ends up funding terrorism worldwide.

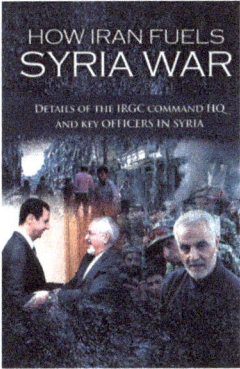

How Iran Fuels Syria War: Details of the IRGC Command HQ and Key Officers in Syria

November 2016, 74 pages

This book examines how the Iranian regime has effectively engaged in the military occupation of Syria by marshaling 70,000 forces, including the Islamic Revolutionary Guard Corps (IRGC) and mercenaries from other countries into Syria; is paying monthly salaries to over 250,000 militias and agents to prolong the conflict; and divided the country into 5 zones of conflict, establishing 18 command, logistics and operations centers.

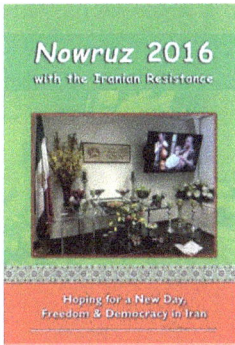

Nowruz 2016 with the Iranian Resistance: Hoping for a New Day, Freedom and Democracy in Iran

April 2016, 36 pages

This book describes Iranian New Year, Nowruz celebrations at the Washington office of Iran's parliament-in-exile, the National Council of Resistance of Iran. The yearly event marks the beginning of spring. It includes select speeches by dignitaries who have attended the NCRIUS Nowruz celebrations.

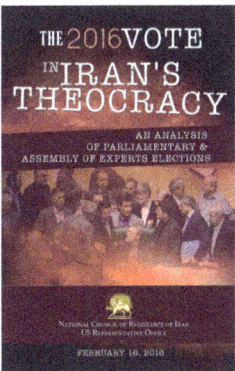

The 2016 Vote in Iran's Theocracy: An analysis of Parliamentary & Assembly of Experts Elections

February 2016, 70 pages

This book examines all the relevant data about the 2016 Assembly of Experts as well as Parliamentary elections ahead of the February 2016 elections. It looks at the history of elections since the revolution in 1979 and highlights the current intensified infighting among the various factions of the Iranian regime.

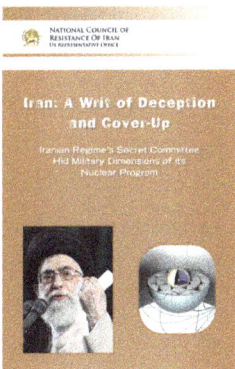

IRAN: A Writ of Deception and Cover-up: Iranian Regime's Secret Committee Hid Military Dimensions of its Nuclear Program

February 2016, 30 pages

The book provides details about a top-secret committee in charge of forging response to the International Atomic Energy Agency (IAEA) regarding the Possible Military Dimensions (PMD) of Tehran's nuclear program, including those related to the detonators called EBW (Exploding Bridge Wire), an integral part of developing an implosion type nuclear device.

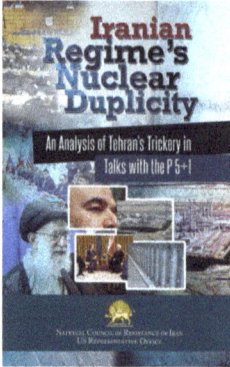

Iranian Regime's Nuclear Duplicity: An Analysis of Tehran's Trickery in Talks with the P 5+1

January 2016, 74 pages

This book examines Iran's behavior throughout the negotiations process in an effort to inform the current dialogue on a potential agreement. Drawing on both publicly available sources and those within Iran, the book focuses on two major periods of intense negotiations with the regime: 2003-2004 and 2013-2015.

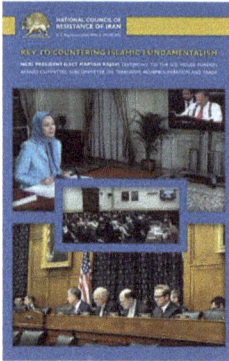

Key to Countering Islamic Fundamentalism: Maryam Rajavi? Testimony To The U.S. House Foreign Affairs Committee

June 2015, 68 pages

Testimony before U.S. House Foreign Affairs Committee's subcommittee on Terrorism, non-Proliferation, and Trade discussing ISIS and Islamic fundamentalism. The book contains Maryam Rajavi's full testimony as well as the question and answer by representatives.

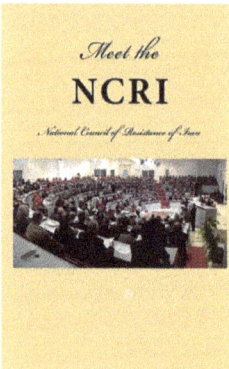

Meet the National Council of Resistance of Iran

June 2014, 150 pages

Meet the National Council of Resistance of Iran discusses what NCRI stands for, what its platform is, and why a vision for a free, democratic, secular, non-nuclear republic in Iran would serve world peace.

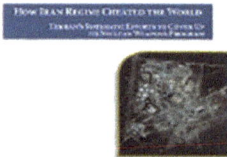

How Iran Regime Cheated the World: Tehran's Systematic Efforts to Cover Up its Nuclear Weapons Program

June 2014, 50 pages

The monograph discusses the Iranian regime's report card as far as it relates to being transparent when addressing the international community's concerns about the true nature and the ultimate purpose of its nuclear program.

6.
ABOUT NCRI-US

National Council of Resistance of Iran-US Representative Office acts as the Washington office for Iran's Parliament-in-exile, which is dedicated to the establishment of a democratic, secular, non-nuclear republic in Iran.

NCRI-US, registered as a non-profit tax-exempt organization, has been instrumental in exposing many nuclear sites of Iran, including the sites in Natanz, and Arak, the biological and chemical weapons program of Iran, as well as its ambitious ballistic missile program.

NCRI-US has also exposed the terrorist network of the Iranian regime, including its involvement in the bombing of Khobar Towers in Saudi Arabia, the Jewish Community Center in Argentina, its fueling of sectarian violence in Iraq and Syria, and its malign activities in other parts of the Middle East.

Visit our website at www.ncrius.org

You may follow us on   twitter   @ncrius

Follow us on   facebook   NCRIUS

You can also find us on   Instagram   NCRIUS

www.ingramcontent.com/pod-product-compliance
Lightning Source LLC
Chambersburg PA
CBHW042333030426
42335CB00027B/3320